So Ya Wanna Marry A Man With Kids?
Really!

Second Edition
ISBN: 978-1-971419-17-6

"You just got engaged to a lovely man,
But he has kids and an ex-wife—it's not as you planned.

Are you sure you want to take this step ahead?
Your life will be way harder than what you've read.

Have you studied the truth about a blended family?
I've appeared to you to show you its reality."

Back in the day when a woman stepped in,
It wasn't from divorce or a husband's sin.

It was when Mom had died — from plague or birth,
Dad grabbed a spinster with questionable worth.

Say "stepmom" and you're shouting, "I'm a mom wannabe!
I'll cook, I'll clean, and pretend, you see."

The word is outdated, the stigma still stands,
From Cinderella to Snow White — stepmoms are damned.

If Cinderella's mom showed up at the ball,
The Evil Queen's fury would've killed them all.

"It's a 50/50 chance for a traditional fam to stay,
But blending families makes it a harder game to play.

Now it's 70% that end in divorce,
Blended families is the worst choice, of course.

More kids, more stress—it's not the best,
Without the right mindset, your love won't pass the test.

Would you gamble your money on a 70/30 bet?
So why risk your heart and money on divorce roulette?"

"'Yes, you can wait and have your own family,
You don't have to join a broken one, can't you see?

They say, 'Ready for marriage? Date a guy with little kids,
He needs a woman to step in where the mother did.'

Hold out for Mr. Right, no kids in sight,
No ex-wife drama to keep you up at night."

Men don't want to pay for a kid that's not theirs,
They're wired to provide and protect their own heirs.

If he's rich and handsome, he can have anyone,
Why pick a single mom? That would be dumb.

They want full freedom, no built-in crew,
No past attachments coming through.

Men do what serves them — that's how they win.
Women still serve men. Let that sink in.

You said you'd never do this — be the second wife,
Join a man with kids and a difficult life.

But now you're thirty-something, tired, and worn,
And that child-free dream feels tattered and torn.

You told yourself, "This isn't the score,
But I'm not young and hot like I was before."

Let me stop you right there — this ain't your plan.
You're just tired... and settling for a man.

Your mama said no. Your grandma begged twice.
Your best friend screamed, "Girl, take my advice!"

The Lyft driver sighed. The cashier just stared.
Even your therapist looked genuinely scared.

The nail lady paused, mid-cuticle trim —
Whispered, "No kids," though her English is slim.

But you still said, "He's worth the fight!"
Like prison sounds fun if the jumpsuit fits right.

Look at Tina — swiped out and sore,
John was a nudist, Steve said, "I'm poly—room for four.

Polyamory, foot pics, conspiracy threads —
One guy lived in a van parked behind his ex's shed.

She thought apps were the worst men alive —
Turns out step-life makes Tinder look like a prize.

Exes, drama, money, and kids —
Silence and wine beat the mess that this is.

Feminism said you can work, hit the gym, get your hair blown,
Nails, friends, hot sex, run the world on your own.

But not, "Congrats, darling, here's his ex and her crew —
Now raise her kids and cut your paycheck in two."

You worked hard for your degree, you fought to get ahead,
Late nights, big dreams — not his child support instead.

Is handing your paycheck to his broken family
Really what a smart, ambitious girl should be?

If you're 1000% sure he's the one, then fine —
But at 99%? Darling, take more time.

If you marry a man with child support and alimony,
Is that the life you really want, honey?

The mother of his children needs money to live,
While you get less and are expected to give.

I know you don't want to hear what is true,
she should have the money more than you.

If he's rich and you don't have to work,
the deal can make sense.
If he's broke, the choice is ridiculously dense.

"Don't be the crazy lady calling the mom 'biological,'
While you wave around the title of 'Stepmom,' illogical.

You're not a 'second mom'—that's not your fight,
You're the Dad's wife, so get the role right.

That outdated term belongs in the lost and found,
With a 70% divorce rate, you probably won't hang
around.

Two moms confuse the kids—what they had was just
fine,
One mom, one dad, and you staying in line!"

When you marry a man with kids, here's what is true:
You're also marrying the mother — she's part of the stew.

You can't make decisions, you can't make the calls —
Another woman's children will never be yours at all.

Those are her children, with your husband in tow,
She's got his money and kids — what do you have to show?

And if you divorce, you're erased from his life,
While he's tied to his children (and her) for life.

It's why this never works, no matter the try —
Blended families weren't meant to exist... unless Mom had to die.

Oh, so you've got kids too? How old, you say?
Just helps me count the therapy hours coming your way.

If yours and his are grown — congrats, that's great.
Still, a guy with no kids is a better mate.

If the kids are young? You're totally screwed.
It's diapers and drama and blended-family feud.

Teenagers? Worse. Now they've got mouths —
Attitude, hormones, and full-blown blowouts.

You can marry the drama and step into his zoo,
Or stay single, sleep in, and do what you do.

If you marry a man with kids, you'll have to join a group,
Where you'll whine and complain about the whole troop.

The women there? They'll show you with glee,
They made a bad choice too, as you'll plainly see.

They cry that the kids don't listen or care,
"The ex is a demon, it's just not fair!"

It's meltdowns, migraines, and bottles of gin,
"But me? I'M A HERO — the problem's with them!"

And yes, you'll have to see a therapist too,
Who silently thinks, "What the hell's wrong with you?"

You rant that the kids are ungrateful and mean,
The ex is a psycho, the worst ever seen.

You swear you're the victim, the saint in this mess,
But you chose the disaster — admit it, confess.

So quit with the whining, the blame, and the doubt,
If you're this damn miserable — then get the fuck out.

Only certain women survive this fate —
And it's not love, it's personality traits.

If you're dependent on a man, if you need his cash,
If you're a people-pleasing doormat who comes in last...

If self-sacrifice is the hill where you'll die —
Congrats, you'll "make it." The rest? Don't even try.

'Cause those are the only people who last in this state,
If that's not you, give the ring back before it's too late.

The Psychology of Why This Fails

1. Invisible Labor
Work full time, now raise his crew?
It's not the 1800s — you didn't have a job too.

2. Attachment & Bonding
You'll never be Mom, don't flatter your head —
That spot's already taken, and she ain't dead.

3. Role Strain & Burnout
Housekeeper, shrink, and a goddess in bed —
You'll lose yourself fast, till "you" is dead.

4. Cognitive Dissonance
"I love his kids like mine!" — shut up, that's fake.
It's just your brain lying for sanity's sake.

You'll call the ex crazy, unstable, insane,
But that's projection to cover your pain.

You feel insecure, so you shift and you blame,
Crown yourself "victim" in a losing game.

It's cognitive dissonance — truths you can't face,
You'll never be mom, you can't take her place.

She's the kids' mother, that role is cement,
So quit screaming "she's crazy" — it's you who's unbent.

Didn't you want love and time for two?
Instead, you got someone who doesn't have time for you.

Women want kisses, affection, a little romance —
He's got ten minutes for sex, not to take you to dance.

Do you want a life feeling lonely and small,
When you could find a man with no baggage at all?

It takes seven years for step-families to blend —
But most tap out before year two ends.

Holidays come and you'll brace for the fight,
Blended fam chaos, nothing feels right.

At Easter you'd rather choke on a Peep,
Than host a blended family and feel like the housekeep.

At Thanksgiving you'd rather slice through your vein,
Than pass the potatoes while swallowing pain.

At Hanukkah you'd rather go up in the menorah flames,
Than fake one more round of fake-family games.

At Christmas you'd rather get fried by the tree,
Than smile at the ex who they'd rather see.

Tell me, darling — is this really your plan?
When you could've picked, a child-free man.

You can't post another woman's kids online,
You say, "I can, they're my husband's, it's fine."

You can post them if he gives you permission,
But you've no legal rights to his addition.

Is it safe to post kids online anyway?
No, it's where pedophiles find their prey.

And you know it's cruel, done only to sting —
Posting another woman's children is a spiteful
thing.

"When your husband dies, the kids get all the
dough,
Though you cared all along, now out you go.

It's the final proof you were never a part
Of a family that already had a start.

You cared for your husband while his kids lived
their life,
But they get all his money—because you're just the
wife.

In a real family, when the dad's laid to rest,
The mom gets the dough, then the kids get the
rest."

A man with no kids? His attention is yours.
Money for steak and vacation tours.

His money? Yours. His time? All in.
Child-free men are a win-win-win.

Sex anytime — anyplace, any space.
Why would you choose a harder life to face?

I've shown millions their blended fate,
They all came back crying, "It's too much to take!"

"I didn't know it'd be this rough!" — oh, please.
It's hard dating single men — and you thought this
would be ease?

You married a man with kids and an ex-wife too...
Did you really think it'd be easier? Are you stupid, boo?

But hey, if you're dead set, then press your luck —
I'm a ghost... I don't give a fuck.

I just wanted to show you — my ghost fam is bliss,
A thousand years strong, I wouldn't settle for less than this.

Our society never celebrates what's whole these days,
They mostly toast broken — or trans and gay ways.

They won't cheer for families still solid, intact,
They clap when it's shattered and call it "progress," in fact.

And here's the question you'd better allow:
Why did your fiancé break his vow?

"It's the end of our journey, thank God it's done,
I hate showing people their future 'blended family' fun.

I'd rather show a killer his future jail cell,
Or an old lady dying alone in a rundown motel.

How about showing a guy getting hit by a bus,
Or a midlife crisis dude losing it —no fuss!

All of that's less depressing, I'm telling you true,
Than a chaotic, crazy blended family zoo."

I know this book has been tough love, but it truly comes from love. I want every woman reading to live a life of peace, joy, and real happiness. Whatever path you choose, make sure it's right for you.

Be kind to yourself. Be kind to others. Keep your eyes open when you make big choices — and don't be afraid to admit when something isn't working. Changing your mind isn't failure, it's wisdom.

Women need each other. We grow stronger when we lift one another up and share what we've learned.

If this book made you think, laugh, or rethink, please leave a review — and share your best piece of advice for other women there. Your words may be exactly what another woman needs before making the biggest decision of her life.

With love,

-G